Titolo | The corona code
Autore | Marco Corona
ISBN | 978-88-27803-43-1

Youcanprint Self-Publishing
Via Roma, 73 - 73039 Tricase (LE) - Italy
www.youcanprint.it
info@youcanprint.it
Facebook: facebook.com/youcanprint.it
Twitter: twitter.com/youcanprintit

Introduction

Here I am ! White apron and hands always covered in flour.

My name is Marco Corona, and I'm sure that most of you have never even heard of me, but on the other hand, at the "Al Fresco" restaurant at the Four Season Hotel in Florence, Italy, I'm a very important person.... and sometimes a star!

What do I do? I've been making pizzas for 25 years!

And what's the big deal? There are hundreds of *"pizzaiolos"*[1], what makes me

---

[1][Translator's note: Throughout text the Italian , pizzaiolo, will be used instead of the English pizza man]

so special, that I actually considered writing a book?

Well, I'm not just an anybody, I 've made pizzas for princes, actors, and VIPs.

So what ? You're in a higher league, but you're still a *pizzaiolo*, not a chef!

Yeah, I get it , only chefs become famous, for now.

Well, let's say, that I'm a pizza chef, not just an anybody.

Above all , I consider myself a researcher , always looking for new tricks and secrets to create the perfect pizza.

Special wheats, new blends of flours and exclusive doughs, that only I can create.

I like to better myself and the products that I offer my clients.

Presumptuous ? No... just self-confident.

Presumptuous are those that brag about skills they don't have.

Since I can't invite all of you to try my pizza, I decided to share my knowledge with the world, the secrets of a perfect pizza dough.

Would you like me to return to my oven?

Share? Why should I ? Nobody shares their secrets. Especially chefs , all notoriously jealous of their "tricks" of the trade.

They will describe a recipe, but it never comes out like they show you, because they NEVER disclose their real secrets!

Each to their own. I, on the other hand, want everyone, professionals and enthusiastic foodies, to be able to learn the secrets of a perfect pizza.

Pizza isn't only my profession and passion, but, also, part of Italy's heritage and culture. Giving the world the perfect pizza , is my dream and goal.

I guess, I'm just different.

I want everyone to able to achieve a perfect pizza dough: easy to digest, healthy and delicious.

Not only! Give them the option to choose whether it should be thin, crispy or soft.
I'm going to teach you about the different types of flours, how to recognize them, and choose the right one.

To make a long story short : I want to share all my skills , not hiding anything! From the simplest , to the more complex chemical reactions.

I want everyone, in the whole world, to become a pizza expert,

 So, let's get started, if you feel like it, and trust me, continue reading, if not... well, your lost. I 'm sure, that sooner or later, my books will become best sellers!

Lack of modesty ? No, self -confidence and determination.

Please excuse me, but I've got to go check my dough....... *later*.

1

I'm going to start by telling you a little about myself.

Don't worry it isn't an autobiography.

To understand why I decided to write this booklet, you need to understand why I love my profession, my thoughts on cooking.

Some go in search of a job, and find it in a pizza restaurant. They learn, get experience, and it becomes their profession.

Maybe, even forever, no matter how good or bad they're at it, it's their JOB.

On the other hand, there are the lucky ones, that were born to do this, for them, it isn't just a "job", but a passion.

I 'm one of them! I knew, even before I started working, that making pizza would be my life.

As a child I remember my grandmother kneading dough, and letting me play with small pieces of it. More than this, I can still smell the aroma, and feel the texture of the dough under my tiny fingers.

I didn't know it at the time, but my senses had chosen my path, I could only follow it.

Why am I telling you this? Well,.... to help you understand, that if you do something with passion, you just don't do it, but you need to go beyond. Cooking is expanding, researching, experimentation, and never being tired of new tastes and techniques.

If it were different, it would only be preparing food, not cooking.

Cooking means being always curious, and, in this, there is no difference between traditional cuisine, nouvelle cuisine or "only" pizza. (the inverted commas are a must!)

Actually pizza, the symbol of Italian cuisine, should be the most studied, because, besides the taste, there are other very important characteristics.

I don't mean the toppings, which depend , for the most, on personal taste or creativity, but the dough, which is the most important part, the one that makes the difference.

Not only the taste and texture have to be taken in consideration, but health issues such as intolerances and digestibility .

" Pizza makes me thirsty"

"I like pizza , but I don't digest it"

"Pizza? I love it , but my stomach bloats after I eat it"

How many times have you heard this? And how many times has it happened to you ?

So , now you know why I'm here.

I'm going to tell you about the results of my research on pizza dough, and teach you how to make a perfect one, every time.

2

I was lucky from the beginning of my career. I started working in our family restaurant in Hungry, where pizza culture was inexistent. As soon as the pizza came out of the oven , it would be garnished with almost anything (HORROR): mayonnaise , sugar, ketchup, you name it!

Thankfully, I was then, exactly as I am today: curious, creative, perfectionist and proud.

A lot of the pizza dough balls ended up in the trash, even though I knew that for my clients, they would have been more than acceptable, but NOT for me.

I kept thinking about my grandmother, and my childhood. What I remembered was the flour she used: its color, texture and aroma. When she kneaded the dough, she always gave us little pieces to play with.

I continued to knead the dough , but that aroma and texture wasn't there. Sometimes we remember facts or images differently , but we never forget an aroma, or at least we always recognize one, and try to reproduce it.

It's similar to the harmony of sounds or colors, if it's there we don't notice it, but when it's not, we do immediately.

Where did this lack of harmony of texture and aromas come from?

The flour.

No doubt.

There were probably other reasons, but, for sure, the flour was the starting point.

And that's where my research, study and experiments began.

Nowadays, it would have been easier, you just need internet, and you can find almost anything, but 25 years ago....

In that year, the first website appeared , obviously, not about pizza!

The information I needed , was hard to find and wasn't available unless you were a biologist or chemist, which I certainly wasn't.

Back then there weren't even schools for *pizzaiolos.*

So, all hands on.

Research, experiments and more research: visits to farms to see firsthand how wheat was grown, and understand its structure.

The first result was: the flour my grandmother used non longer existed, at least, not with the same characteristics.

Why wasn't it easy to find?

The reasons are multiple, and a lot of space would be needed to explain them.

The most obvious was economic: the manipulation of grains to increase productivity.

Wheat and its precious germ have changed through the decades because of manipulations (this is an important topic that will be discussed in another booklet), and this, naturally changed the grains original components (proteins and starch), causing the constant diffusion of gluten intolerance.

A this point, it dawned on me, that my research needed to follow two different, but parallel paths.

First, I needed to study the different types of flours, in order to be able to choose the appropriate ones.

Second, I needed to understand the chemical reactions that happen to the ingredients in the dough.

This was the only way I would be able to understand the ingredients and develop the best method of combining them in order to obtain the result I was hoping for: a dough that was light, leavened, easy to digest, and that would not cause intolerances.

In a nutshell, make a pizza, everyone could eat without problems, but also recreate the aromas of my childhood.

3

The first fundamental step was studying the wheat germ structure, not the easiest, considering that I had no chemistry !

I know, boring, I'll make it easy and, as short as possible, just enough to follow the rest!

Familiarizing with the wheat germ and its structure, will help you understand the different types of flour, and their best use.

Like we say in Italy, you need to walk , before you can run: the first step is hard , but the most important.

So, now, I'm going to start by explaining the composition of the soft wheat grain
(soft flour).

As I mentioned before, a good knowledge of the key facts, will help you understand the composition and differences of the various types of flours.

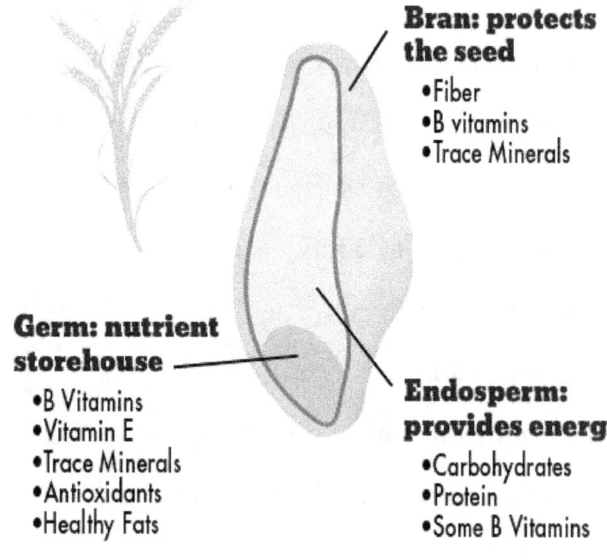

The wheat grain is composed of three main parts:

- The bran (external layer) : made of vegetable fibers, protein, minerals and vitamins.
- Endosperm, starch (inner layer)
- Germ, rich in vitamins and minerals and the embryo of the new plant.

Milling of the entire grain gives whole wheat flour.

Grinding and sifting the grains gives us plain flour (the most refined without traces of germ and bran).

The different levels of sifting and milling (i.e. separating the germ and bran) , gives us the different types of flours:

- Whole wheat
- TYPE 2   (partial whole wheat)
- TYPE 1   (partial whole wheat)
- TYPE 0   (plain flour)
- TYPE 00 (cake flour)

(in order of refinement, according to Italian classifications).

Type 1 is the most noble of all flours, it maintains all its nutrients and most of the germ. Only the hardest part of the bran is eliminated, making it easier to digest.

4

At this point, I had become familiar with wheat and its anatomy, and the broad categories of flour... and now?

I just started walking, or better crawling, but the finish line was still a long way away.

I got another stroke of luck! After leaving the restaurant in Hungry, I found work in Austria, thinking that anything would due, as long as I could continue my research.

I would have never imagined that the owner had been a bread-maker, not only, better still, a Neapolitan bread-maker !

A professional, who had a practical knowledge of dough making , and was just as curious and scrupulous as I.

We worked together, talking and comparing experiences. My brain was like a sponge, absorbing and storing, for later use, all the knowledge, knowhow, ideas, this incredible man was willing to share with me.

Those were wonderful years, spent surrounded by the aroma of the oven and great conversations, while I continued to research grain growing methods, and the composition of different types of flours.

I discovered that, besides the broad categories of flours, there were other variables regarding the strength of the flours, notions that were unknown outside professional circles.

Naturally a little chemistry would have been helpful, but my curiosity and stubbornness , compensated the lack of knowledge. Thanks to this, I was able to learn and understand concepts, up till then, completely out of my reach.

Some of you might ask themselves, why I wasted so much time studying.

Well, the answer to that question is simple: to discover the secret to make a perfect pizza dough, you need an in depth knowledge of the chemical reactions that occur by blending flour, water and yeast, and what's going to happen afterwards.

Therefore the concepts of gluten mesh, enzymes, starch and protein, have to become familiar, in the same way that a painter is familiar with the various techniques like oil painting, watercolor, acrylic and charcoal sketching, in order to create a masterpiece.

Research and knowledge are the fundamentals!

These are often taken for granted, or overlooked, but are necessary, otherwise the end result will always be mediocre .

Acquiring a good knowledge of the chemical processes was challenging, but it made me realize that I was on the right track to reach my goal.

I know this was kind of boring, but why should I suffer alone?

5

Having a good understanding of the chemical reactions is fundamental, not only, in order to choose the right flours, but also to control the leavening process and to make sure the dough is used properly.

All flours (further for the different types) contain two protein substances, Glutenin and Gliadin, which, mixed with water and worked into a dough, give origin to Gluten[2]

---

[2] Gluten is mixture of two proteins present in cereal grains, especially wheat, which is responsible for the elastic texture of the dough.

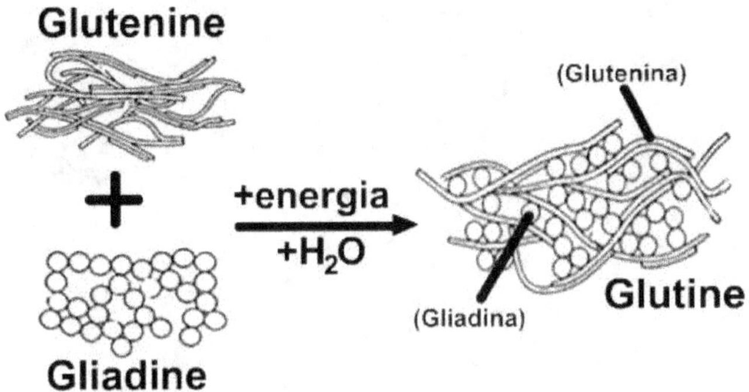

To make it simple, these two proteins, mixed with water, and kneaded into a dough, are activated, forming an elastic net called gluten mesh.

The gluten mesh [3] can be more or less strong for various reasons, but for the most part, it depends on how much protein is in the wheat.

---

[3] The Gluten Mesh is the framework of elastic Gluten strands that hold together dough, traps air bubbles, and gives bread structure.

You might have noticed that supermarkets offer a large range of flours, besides the broad categories, already mentioned.

You may have seen flours with a W followed by a number.

What does that W mean ?

The W indicates the specific STRENGTH and quality of the gluten, i.e. the ability to absorb water. This also influences its leavening capacity.

It's important to be familiar with these categories, in order to choose the right flour.

Following is a list of flours divided according to their strength:

- between W 90 and W160 (weak flours)
- between W 160 and W250 (medium flours)
- between W 250 and W310 (strong flours)
- between W310 and W400 (special flours like Manitoba)

The type of flour and its strength will influence all the steps, from the kneading process, leavening time, and quantity of water needed.

At this point, in my quest, I had learned a lot and gathered a lot of information. But I still hadn't found the answers to those fundamental questions (why is piazza hard to digest? why does it make you thirsty,? why does it make your stomach bloat?), these kept drumming in my brain.

I knew that, what I had learned so far, wasn't enough, I had to carry on, in order to reach my goal.

I constantly thought about those pizza dough balls, that I discarded in Hungry. Beautiful, soft and puffy, they filled me with pride, but, as soon as I tried to roll them out, they would deflate.

As soon as they came in contact with the rolling pin or just my hands, they would pop like a balloon ! They were impossible to shape, I 'd pull one side and the other would snap back....frustrating !

I realized that having learned about wheat structure, chemical processes and, flours, wasn't enough.

I was missing something fundamental, in order to achieve the ideal pizza dough.

I needed to recreate the aroma and texture of my grandmother's dough.

6

Yes, there was secret ... something hidden!

Thinking about sugars, starch, enzymes etc.. I recalled all those problems some had, eating pizza.

Then I remembered a trip to Naples, and a local expression " *sei una pizza* " , which is used to define a person who is boring, i.e. hard to digest.

Often we don't stop to think about certain common expressions, and where they come from, but this one probably derived from a characteristic inherent to pizza : that it's hard to digest!

So, studying the digestive process, became a must, in order to achieve my perfect piazza dough.

Don't worry... non another lecture. I've been boring enough, with all the chemistry and formulas.

To make a long story short, the stomach's main job is to transform the complex elements that we ingest, into simple ones, easy to assimilate .

The digestive process begins ,when the stomach starts to break down these complex elements, and ends when it's done.

In a pizza dough a lot of things occur: chemical reactions and transformations.

As soon as the flour is mixed with water, the first chemical reaction takes place: for example the starches and proteins start to turn into simple sugars and amino acids.

This is a slow process and needs time to complete its cycle, while on the other hand, yeast works quickly. So we see a nice puffy dough, and think it's ready to go into the oven.

This is the big mistake!

This is what few people know, even professionals.

There is a specific step, that is fundamental, but often unknown or overlooked.

It's called the MATURING of the dough.

It's crucial in order to obtain a light and digestible dough.

Why? Easy : this gives the dough enough time to complete its chemical processes, and break down the elements. Therefore it goes into the oven "pre-digested".

The pizza has already broken down the complex elements into simple ones, and will not continue "leavening" in our stomach.

Every process will have been completed, and it won't deflate, when it's handled .

Yeast, not only allows the dough to rise, but also ferment, and this must be taken into consideration.

And people say : be a *pizzaiolo*! As if it were that simple! It depends on how you do it...

enough chitchat. Now, a short summery of what has been said, and then it's time to put all this into practice. About time, getting hungry, aren't you?

7

Ok... so, after years of studies and research, checking and double-checking, I can now explain the three MAIN phases needed to make a perfect dough: tasty, fragrant and digestible .

It won't make you thirsty, or bloat you stomach, or be hard to digest.

I had also, finally, found that aroma, I spent ages trying to recreate.

Before going into the oven , our dough has to complete three phases:

- leavening
- fermentation

- maturation

LEAVENING

At the leavening stage, the gluten creates a kind of grind (called gluten mesh) that detains the starches and gasses that develop.

FERMENTATION

Fermentation is the chemical process that takes place in absence of oxygen. The yeast changes its metabolic process into alcohol and CO_2.

MATURATION

Maturation begins as soon as you start preparing the dough, and continues till it's placed in the oven.

A lot of changes take place during this phase. For example the starches turn into simple sugars.

The maturation of the dough is similar to the hanging of meat.

How long each phase lasts, depends on the type of flour used.

Lower the value of the W (weak flours) the faster, the higher the value of the W (medium flours), the longer.

Remember that this last phase (maturation), is the most important for a digestible and a high quality pizza.

With this basic knowledge, having selected the flour, we'll know exactly what to do.

We'll be able to make an excellent pizza in 4/5 hours with a low W, or in 48 hours with a high W, using the fridge.

 The fridge?

Yes your normal, everyday household refrigerator !

The best way to be sure the leavening and maturation processes, take place at the same speed, you need to slow down the leavening process. This can be achieved by maintaining the dough at a low temperature, blocking the action of the yeast.

So, if you place your dough in the fridge at a temperature between 2° and 6° C. (the temperature of most household refrigerators), the leavening process will be slowed down, allowing it to work at the same speed as all the other processes.

This is an important step, that I need to explain in depth, because it's practically unknown.

8

Maturation is a combo of reactions and biochemical processes that start as soon as you mix water and flour.

While kneading the dough, the flour's starch and proteins are attacked by enzymes, that turn them, slowly, into simple sugars and amino acids.

This takes place in various phases, and needs time to complete itself.

To understand this concept, let's compare it to our digestive system.

When we chew food, our saliva releases an enzyme, that breaks down macro-molecules into smaller ones. Starch is broken down and turns into simple sugars and more.

These chemical reactions take place thanks to the presence of water, therefore in hydrolysis.

Hydrolysis is the chemical breakdown of a compound thanks to the presence of water.

This is a slow process, so a good amount of water is needed.

That's why, we get thirsty, after eating pizza. If a dough hasn't completed all the phases, especially maturation, it will continue to do so in our body, stimulating our thirst, in order to obtain the liquid needed.

On the other hand, a mature dough, not only is easy to digest, but has other, surprising characteristics:

- it won't bloat in your stomach (all the chemical reaction are completed)

- it's fragrant (I know..... but it's important!)

- when it come out of the oven , it will have a beautiful amber color thanks to the caramelized sugars , due to the "Maillard reaction"

- it can be , easily digested by those that have a gluten intolerance (not celiac disease , of course, trust me I tried it on myself)

This said, don't you think it's time that we get down to work, and prepare a great pizza together?

Yes, all together, without a wood burning oven or professional machinery .

When I say "together" I mean everyone: chefs, *pizzaiolos*, housewives or just pizza lovers.

Today we are making pizza, so gather the ingredients, and let's get started!

9

First step: choose the flour, the amount of water needed , depends on its strength (W) Following are the right quantities for the different types of flour.

Serves two to three

Weak flours w 90 - w160

- 250 gr. cold water

- 10 gr. salt

- 1 gr. brewer's yeast

- 10 gr. extra virgin olive oil

- 490 gr. (approx.) flour

Medium flours w 160 - w250

250   gr. cold water

- 10 gr. salt

- 1 gr. brewer's yeast

- 10 gr. extra virgin olive oil

- 470 gr. (approx.) flour

Strong flours w 250 – w 310

- 250 gr. cold water

- 10 gr. salt

- 1 gr. brewer's yeast

- 10 gr. extra virgin olive oil

- 440 gr. (approx.) flour

Manitoba flour, w 400 or higher, will be the topic of a future booklet, because it has very specific procedures.

The quantity of flour is approximate because the aim is to obtain the right consistency.

HOMEMADE PIZZA
METHOD

SERVES 2 TO 3

- 250 gr water
- 1 gr. brewer's yeast
- 10 gr. salt
- 10 gr. extra virgin olive oil
- 430 gr. flour (type 1 - 250 W)

Place cold water in a large bowl, add the

yeast and dissolve. Add the olive oil and salt. Gently combine, adding the flour a little at a time.

As soon as the dough comes together ,
start kneading with your hands.

Turn out dough on a smooth, clean surface,
and continue kneading.

Shape into 2 balls, and place each into clean bowl, cover with plastic wrap.

The bowls should be three times larger than the dough balls. Place in fridge.

Resting time:

- Weak flour W   5/6 hours at room temperature.
- Medium four W , place in fridge an hour after forming the dough balls. After 24 hours, at 3° to 5° C, remove from fridge, and leave out to reach room temperature (approx. 2 to 4 hours), roll out
- Strong flour W, 48 hours, same procedure as the medium.

Roll out the dough:

Grease a nonstick, 30 cm. pizza tin with olive oil.

Place the bowl, with the prepared piazza dough, upside down, on the tin. This way the dough will be slightly greased as well.

Flatten slowly and delicately, with finger tips. Let rest 20 to 40 minutes, before placing in pre-heated oven.

Baking and topping

- Pre-heat oven 230°/250° C.
- Drizzle the pizza dough with a little olive oil, and place on lowest oven shelf and bake for 5-7 minutes.
- Move to middle shelf and bake another 5-7 minutes

- Remove from oven and garnish with your favorite toppings, (tomato, mozzarella cheese, basil)

- Return to oven for 5 minutes.

Your homemade pizza is ready, fresh , fragrant and easy to digest.

Who
is
this man?

Marco Corona has been employed for several years at the Four Season Hotel in Florence, Italy, working alongside the Star Chef Vito Mollica [4] , who has always

---

[4] In photo left to right : Vito Mollica, Franco Pepe , Marco Corona

encouraged him to continue his studies on flours.

Article in local paper about the hotel's Pizza Restaurant "Al Fresco" and its VIP guests .

LA NAZIONE

FIRENZE

Four Seasons: martedì 6 giugno evento di riapertura di Al Fresco con Antica Corte Pallavicina e Laurent Perrier

Four Seasons Hotel Firenze dà il benvenuto alla stagione estiva con la riapertura di "Al Fresco", oasi immersa nel Giardino della Gherardesca. Ospiti d'eccezione per la serata inaugurale martedì 6 giugno, Massimo e Luciano Spigaroli, da generazioni specializzati nell'allevamento d'eccellenza di suini nella loro Azienda Agricola Antica Corte Pallavicina e produttori dei migliori salumi della bassa parmense – il loro culatello di Zibello è apprezzato da nomi come Carlo d'Inghilterra e Alain Ducasse. In occasione della riapertura di Al Fresco cureranno un aperitivo con le loro eccellenze, seguito da un menù a "a sei mani" insieme allo Chef di Four Seasons Vito Mollica. L'evento inaugurale, a partire dalle 20, avrà un costo di 90 euro a persona, bevande incluse, e sarà rallegrato da una selezione di Champagne a cura di Laurent-Perrier. La Trattoria Al Fresco anche quest'anno proporrà le eccellenze di carne e pesci preparati sul josper grill e pizze dai sapori unici, con impasti a lievitazione lenta, per garantirne la digeribilità, realizzati con farine biologiche selezionate personalmente dal pizzaiolo Marco Corona e ottenute dai migliori grani teneri macinati a pietra. Previsto anche anche il servizio di pizza-take away.

Al Fresco
Four Seasons Hotel Firenze, Borgo Pinti, 99
Apertura: dal 1 di giugno tutti giorni dalle ore 12.00 – 18.30, ore 19.00 – 23.00
Per informazioni e prenotazioni: 055 2626460,
alfresco@fourseasons.com,
www.ilpalagioristorante.it

Marco Corona's pizzas are described as unique and made with high quality organic flours, which he personally selects.

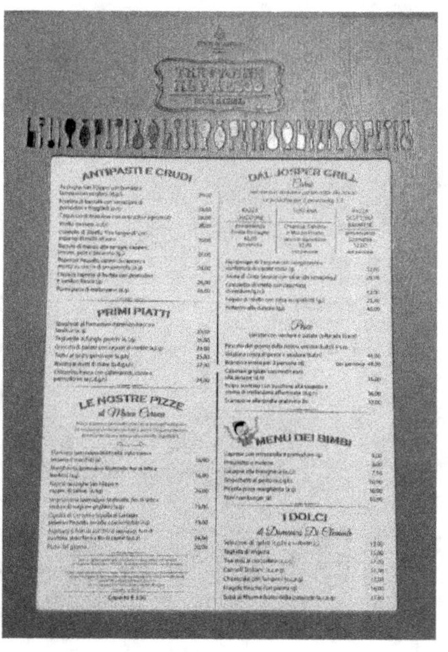

Besides the classic pizza, a selection of pizzas with seasonal products are offered.

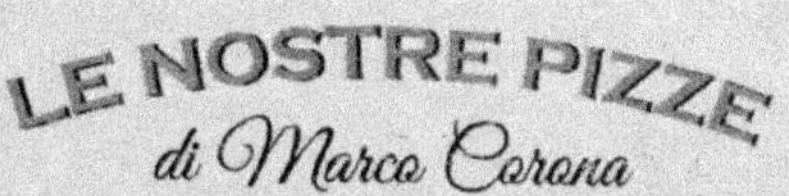

Because of his achievements, Marco Corona
has been listed amongst the best *pizzaiolos*
of Italy, in the latest editions of the
Gambero Rosso guides (a specialized

publication that lists the top restaurants
and chefs in Italy).

Al Fresco

b.go Pinti, 99
TEL. 0552626401
CHIUSO SEMPRE APERTO; APERTO DA
GIUGNO A FINE SETTEMBRE
COPERTI 80
PREZZI PIZZA DA 16 A 24 EURO
CARTE DI CREDITO TUTTE

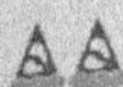 Pizza all'Italiana

È stato lungimirante lo chef Vito Mollica, quando ha deciso di introdurre la pizza nel menu della trattoria Al Fresco. Così nel lussuoso Four Seasons Hotel, circondati dal parco della Gherardesca e coccolati da un servizio a cinque stelle, si può gustare una tonda di qualità e d'autore (per adesso solo nei mesi estivi). Il pizzaiolo Marco Corona si dedica a un incessante lavoro di ricerca, mantenendo una costante sinergia con Mollica (che cura pure la proposta del ristorante Il Palagio, anch'esso interno all'albergo). L'impasto è a base di farine biologiche piemontesi e toscane macinate a pietra, a cui viene aggiunta quella di riso, esaltate da una lunga maturazione con preimpasto poolish. La cottura è in forno elettrico con pietra refrattaria. Nel menu non mancano le classiche Marinara, Margherita e Napoli, affiancate da varianti stagionali come quella con asparagi, fiori di zucchina, stracchino e blu di capra. La pizza signature è la Cipolla di Certaldo, con cipolla toscana, peperoni Piquillo, cacioricotta e borzillo lucano (omaggio alle origini dello chef). Nell'attesa si possono ordinare cocktail dal bar della piscina e alcuni piatti sfiziosi come il vitello tonnato o l'insalata di baccalà. Dalla carta dei vini un'interessante selezione di etichette.

Al Fresco

b.go Pinti, 99
TEL. 0552626401
CHIUSO SEMPRE APERTO; APERTO DA
GIUGNO A FINE SETTEMBRE
COPERTI 80
PREZZI PIZZA DA 19 A 24 EURO
CARTE DI CREDITO TUTTE
www.fourseasons.com/it/florence/
dining/restaurants/al_fresco

 Pizza all'Italiana

Una pizza di qualità nello splendido giardino di un hotel di lusso: a Firenze è possibile, anche se, per ora, solo in estate. Il prezzo non è modico, ma siamo in un Four Season Hotel e si mangia all'aperto circondati dal secolare Parco della Gherardesca coccolati da un servizio impeccabile. Le pizze nascono dalla sinergia con la cucina stellata dello chef Vito Mollica. A mettere le mani in pasta è Marco Corona, pizzaiolo di origini siculo-salentine con esperienze in Italia e all'estero. Il suo stile è frutto di contaminazioni: farine biologiche macinate a pietra, preimpasto poolish per una lunga maturazione e cottura in forno elettrico con pietra refrattaria per una pizza dal cornicione gonfio ma che si discosta dalla napoletana per l'interno meno elastico. Sempre in carta le tradizionali Marinara, Margherito e Napoli, seguono il ritmo delle stagioni la Vegetariana e quella con asparagi, fiori di zucchina, stracchino e salmone affumicato. Di concerto con la cucina, la Four Cheeses con gorgonzola e noci, marzolino e mostarda di fichi, caprino e mostarda d'uva, taleggio e pere; e la Cipolla di Certaldo con cipolla di Certaldo, friggitelli, scamorza affumicata e borzillo lucano, che coniuga il territorio toscano con le origini lucane dello chef. Per accompagnare si possono ordinare vini dalla ricca carta del ristorante Il Palagio. Pizze solo la sera.

DA NON PERDERE
Margherita, Four Cheeses
e Cipolla di Certaldo

Thanks to his professionalism, he was hired as a consultant for the opening of an important Italian restaurant in Egypt, by a client who had simply eaten one of his pizzas.

الشركة المصرية لتجارة أدوات المائدة
EGYPTIAN TABLETOP TRADING COMPANY
المركز الرئيسي

LOFT

In the near future, he will be working as a consultant in other countries, where he will be in charge, not only of the restaurant but also of the training the staff.

Recently, an important article appeared in a famous Japanese blog "CreaWeb" that went viral around the world. Marco would like to take this opportunity to thank the

photographer , Ryoko Fujihara [5]

For this article go to:

http://crea.bunshun.jp/arti

cles/-/13739

translated from the Italian by Renata Petracca

---

[5] **Ryoko Fujiwara** lives in Florence. Professional photographer and writer. After working in Tokyo , she fell in love with Italy 's cuisine and sunshine , and is now working here, writing and capturing the landscape.
https://www.facebook.com/chococogogo

*"Not any pizza, **THIS** pizza!*

In the next booklets

Hard wheat, rice,
spelt, rye, corn.
Let's learn how to
recognize and mix
different flours

Deep pan, thin,
soft or crisp?
How to achieve
the best result
and never fail.

Finito di stampare nel mese di Dicembre 2017
per conto di Youcanprint *Self-Publishing*

www.ingramcontent.com/pod-product-compliance
Lightning Source LLC
Chambersburg PA
CBHW051345150726
48000CB00003B/1058